Table of Contents

Introduction to Boxers

If you're looking for a canine best friend, look no further. Any Boxer owner will tell you that these dogs will quickly become you greatest admirer and best friend. The Boxer's worried look is just a ploy: he's a joyful and friendly dog, seemingly without a worry in the world. They are truly unique in their playful, friendly, and loving characteristics, and they will let you know just how much they crave your attention.

Loyal and goofy, Boxers are smart and almost seem like humans with their curiosity and patience. They certainly seem to believe they are humans sometimes, as they are both stubborn and intelligent. Boxers need an owner who they can respect and love, and someone who will be an alpha. They love playing games and learning new tricks, and they learn even faster when edible treats are involved. If you shower your Boxer with attention, love, exercise, and interaction, they will gladly reward you with lifelong companionship and admiration.

Not only are their personalities fun and happy, but they are also handsome creatures. The Boxers head is his most distinctive feature, with a chiseled square jaw, sweet brown eyes, and an expressive forehead. Despite being bred to be a working dog, these dogs love being with their families and will stick to you like velcro. Boxers of all ages retain their puppy-like curiosity and lovable silliness until their last days.

There are a few aspects of the Boxer puppy and dog traits that are important to consider before you buy; we'll cover all that and more in this book.

This book will help you learn about Boxer puppies, their traits, temperament, challenges, qualities, what to look for, and how best to train them as they grow through puppyhood to adulthood.

Enjoy! We trust this will prove to be helpful to you as you consider this wonderful and loyal breed.

History of Boxer Breed

The Boxer belongs to the Molosser dog group, with ancestors that were first bred near Greece and Albania as far back as the 4th century BC. Molosser-type dogs were considered valuable, and even had depictions in cuneiform in Babylon. Other dogs that were bred from the original Molossers include search and rescue dogs, such as the Newfoundland and the Saint Bernard, and also guard dogs, such as the Mastiff.

The Boxer is thought to be bred from the now extinct Bullenbeisser, a Mastiff-like dog, and the Bulldogs brought in from Great Britain. The Bullenbeisser had been a hunting dog, used for bear, wild boar, and deer. Eventually, faster dogs were bred and favored, but it is accepted by many experts that the Brabanter Bullenbeisser was a direct ancestor of today's Boxer. Prior to the time of Bullenbeisser, there is evidence that Boxers may also be direct descendants of a fighting dog of the high valleys of Tibet.

16th and 17th century tapestries show scenes of boar and stag hunting, with hunting dogs in tow. The dogs depicted are the Spanish Alano and the Matin de Terceira or Perro do Presa, which are regarded as either ancestors of the Boxer or they may just share a common ancestor. There may even be a hint of heritage from a terrier strain in the Boxers we know and love today.

In 1894, the Boxer as a breed was stabilized by Friedrich Robert, R. Höpner, and Elard König and they put it on exhibition at a dog show. The first Boxer Club was founded in 1896 and soon after the first Boxer breed standard was developed, and it has not seen many changes to this day.

After its introduction to other parts of Europe and the United States around the turn of the 20th century, the dog began to gain popularity. During World War I, the Boxer was trained and used for military work. They were valuable to the cause, acting as an attack and guard dog, valuable messenger dog, and a pack-carrier. After World War II, the Boxer became popular throughout the world. Returning soldiers would take them home and they became a favorite companion and guard dog.

Some experts believe that the name "Boxer" derived from the breed's tendency to play by standing on its hind legs and "boxing" with its front paws. Author Andrew H. Brace of Pet Owner's Guide to the Boxer believes that this theory is not very plausible, as "it's unlikely that a nation so permeated with nationalism would give to one of its most famous breeds a name so obviously Anglicized.

Historical evidence and German linguistics have found that the earliest written source for the Boxer dog appears in The German Dictionary of Foreign Words. It cites an author named Musäus writing "daß er aus Furcht vor dem großen Baxer Salmonet ... sich auf einige Tage in ein geräumiges Packfaß ... absentiret hatte". In the late 18th century, the terms "baxer" and "boxer" were equal. In German, the verb "boxen" means "to box, punch or jab", with "boxer" as the noun form. In the Bavarian dialect, the term Boxl (also Buxn or Buchsen) means "short (leather) trousers" or "underwear". Brace also stated that many other theories explaining the origin of the breed name exist. He favors one in particular, that suggests that the smaller Bullenbeisser were also known as "Boxl" and that the modern name Boxer is just a corruption of that word.

Regardless, we think the name and physical aspects of this breed fit quite well.

Development

The overall development of a Boxer is determined by the mother's temperament. Puppies are taught how to interact with the world by learning from their mothers and kind and wise breeders determine the mother's temperament. If the mothers are nurtured to be fearful and aggressive or happy and relaxed, the puppy will learn these traits. It's wise to choose a loving and knowledgeable breeder is very important.

Once a breeder and puppy has been chosen or you choose to be a breeder yourself, you must know that newborn puppies of all breeds sleep almost 24 hours a day. During this neo-natal phase that lasts roughly two weeks, they will make little sounds, when hungry or upset, and the mother will help them accordingly. They need so much time to sleep to continue development, and the mothers of the puppies will remind them that they must sleep.

During this time, the puppies should be handled by people in order to begin and maintain socialization with humans. Holding them very gently, perpendicular to the ground with their heads down and their back in the palm of your hand is very important for neurological stimulation. Gentle petting and speaking softly or cooing to the puppy helps develop positive social habits throughout their life. If you are still in the market for a breeder, you will want to look for a breeder who handles their pups from the very beginning.

Throughout the transitional period, 14-21 days after birth, the puppy will become more active. They will learn to walk instead of crawl, playing with their brother and sisters, and they'll learn how to wag their tails. The puppies should be getting individual human attention, including petting, holding, and introduction of toys and speaking and/or cooing. At this time they can also be brought into different rooms, like kitchens or living rooms, in order to experience the sounds, smells, and textures. Assorted flooring like carpet, vinyl, wood, or tile will help stimulate their tactile senses. This stage of understanding their world is incredibly important for the puppy's stimulation.

Their first awareness period, 21-28 days after their birth, the puppies have been able to use all of their senses. All kinds of sights, sounds, smell, movements, and vibrations should be introduced. At this stage fear has not yet developed, so getting startled may happen, but they should be able to relax without intervention from humans. This is very important because it teaches them that they will be okay, and it is something they must be able to do the rest of their lives.

At this time, puppies will begin to play fight, bark, and bond to each other and to humans. The mother will also start to interject in order to discipline them. It is important to let the mother discipline to teach them the dog rules of dominance and submission. Food is slowly introduced and weaning begins at this stage. Problems with social skills in the future can be made during this time, especially if the pup is removed from the litter due to illness or injury. Proper interaction with other dogs during this time is necessary to ensure positive and normal social skills.

During the second awareness period, 28-35 days after birth, the pups should be removed individually from the litter for short periods of time and given attention. This will help create independence and the ability to build trusting relationships with people. This problem will also help prevent problems with separation anxiety later on. Bringing individual puppies to new places and showing them new smells and sounds helps them adjust and adapt more rapidly, especially when getting adopted into a new home. Without the littermates to help, they won't have the chance to solve any issues or correct any anxiety that may arise.

5-12 weeks after the birth, the puppies' curiosity is at its height. It is important to encourage this curiosity and give the puppies a lot of stimulation and interaction with other animals to ensure that they will be well rounded. It is important that the pup doesn't see cats, birds, or other animals as 'prey' or 'toys'. It would also be good to expose the pup to children, and how to play with children.

The pup will usually be adopted somewhere in this period, because the pup should have learned enough to live without its mother or litter-mates, and bonding at this time is very important. Lots of individual attention is crucial in this time period. Make sure to be gentle, have fun with them, and constantly handle the puppy. Sometimes puppies will show more interest in another dog, instead of the new owner. If this happens, try to keep them separated from the dog for a longer time. Alternately, if they shy away from another dog and come to you, leave them alone with the dog more often. This will help deepen and balance the bond between you and your new pup. The pup will need to balance human and dog social skills.

Puppies will experience an increase of fearfulness when brought to a new home. It's important that the new owner does not try to 'fix' this fearfulness, but instead allow the puppy to become accustomed to their new life. Try not to soothe a scared puppy, and just go about your day while letting the puppy adjust, as they will. This will teach them to be independent and it will not reinforce their fear. Also try to give them a lot of new experiences to encourage curiosity, and don't be afraid of startling them.

The pup's reactive tendencies will be established during these weeks, especially how to react to fear. Don't tip toe around when the puppy is sleeping, and also don't avoid loud people or places. It is important for them to understand the world this way, and to encourage bravery and curiosity. During this fear stage, being visibly angry, shouting or hurting the puppy will have lasting affects throughout its life. Scolding and discipline must be somewhat gentle, and follow by encouraging a good behavior with praise and tenderness. When a pup is taught not to be fearful with love and affection, he will have a happier personality.

Also during this time, make sure to give them baths to ensure that bath-time is not a scary experience, teach them tricks such as how to sit, come, and let go. The pup must also learn bite inhibition and how to be gentle. Allow your pup to follow you and watch you go about your day. Make eye contact, talk to him, pet him, and involve him in your activities as much as you can. This will not only deepen the bond, but your pup will love and respect you just that much more.

For up to 6 months after birth, the pup will be in the independence stage. This period is notoriously frustrating for a new owner, and especially those who have never raised a puppy. The puppy is learning exactly what being independent means and they will stubbornly push these boundaries. The puppy will begin to play "games", like running away when off leash, biting, refusing to listen or obey, fighting the leash, and/or just downright ignoring you. Although these behaviors are normal for this age, they can be incredibly irritating.

Make sure to enforce the rules of gentleness and obedience, even when you feel they are falling on deaf ears. Still play and interact with the pup, give them ample social interactions. Eventually your hard and diligent work will pay off, and the pup will become easier to handle. Do not allow dominance, possessiveness, destructiveness, marking, or timidity from the puppy, and you will have yourself a very happy and obedient dog.

After that stubborn phase, you will have a bit of peace and quiet. The pre-teen stage that occurs at the ages of 7-12 months will have the pup listening better. They should continue to be socialized extensively, encouraging playfulness and energy, but also teach them not to jump on people and to stay until you say it's okay to come. Some owners call this the "calm before the teenage storm", so take full advantage of basic obedience training. During this stage, they will also be cutting their adult teeth, so make sure to provide proper chew toys, or else they will be chewing on anything they can get their teeth on.

The next and last stage for development is the adolescence stage, which happens at about 1 year old. Your puppy will become very intense about everything at this age, as he now has near complete understanding of his world. He will try to assert dominance, forget about playing gently, and will have a need to exercise heavily. If you've chosen not to have your pup fixed, this is the age of sexual maturity as well and attraction to the opposite sex will become troublesome no matter which gender.

Make sure to reinforce your rules, because the beginning of this stage will have your teenage dog testing you constantly. At times you will see your pup having the emotional maturity of a toddler, but try not to get frustrated because it is quite normal and will soon pass. By having your household rules constantly reinforced and ingrained, you will have fewer and fewer problems with stubbornness.

By 2-3 years old, your dog will now be settled in his prime. All your hard work in training and reinforcing with love will be rewarded with a well-behaved best friend and constant companion. Their energies, personalities, and behaviors will be stabilized, and will remain so for the majority of their lives. An older dog may get grumpy, clingy, or sad for many different reasons, so it is important to have regular vet check-ups throughout their lives.

Physical Characteristics

Boxers are most known for their distinctive heads and expressive eyes. Their mouths have a protruding lower jaw that goes beyond the upper jaw and bends slightly upwards. This is also called an under bite or an undershot bite. Since its head is the Boxer's most distinctive feature, show standards suggest that it is important to have a ratio of 1:3 of the length of the muzzle to the whole of the head.

Docking and cropping used to be common occurrences for the Boxer breed. They would have their ears cropped and their tails docked routinely. Due to pressure form multiple veterinary associated, animal rights groups, and the general public, these painful traditions have been prohibited. To anticipate the bans, Boxers were bred for a naturally short tail and these dogs were accepted in the Kennel Club registry in 1998.

The Boxer's coat is short, dense, and very smooth. Only a little grooming is needed, but if your dog's coat is rough, his health may be in turmoil. The recognized colors are fawn and brindle, frequently with a white underbelly and feet. The white markings are called "flash", and they often extend onto the face and/or neck. Fawn Boxers range from a light tan to a dark mahogany.

Brindle Boxers have black stripes on a fawn background, but sometimes there is more brindling, and it looks more like there are fawn stripes on a black body. The breed standard doesn't allow heavily brindled Boxers, and the fawn background must be clearly contrasted.

White Boxers have a coat that is more than 1/3 white. They are neither rare nor albino, and about 23% of all Boxers are born white. Genetically, these dogs are actually fawn or brindle with excessive white markings overlying their coats. White Boxers are at a higher risk for skin cancers. Also 18% of all white Boxers will be deaf in one or both ears. In the past, white Boxers were routinely euthanized, but today most breeders will place white puppies in pet homes as long as they agree to spay/neuter. They are prohibited from breeding, but can compete in events such as obedience and agility. They also do well as therapy or service dogs.

Health: Common Ailments and Preventative Measures

As with all breeds, it's important to know some of the more common ailments, and preventative measures that can be taken as you consider which breed is best for you.

Cardiac Problems

The most common heart problems that affect Boxers are the aortic stenosis, affecting the aortic valve, arrhythmia, and cardiomyopathy. Symptoms of heart diseases may come in the form of exercise intolerance, coughing after exercise, fainting, or sudden collapse. Some Boxers may show no signs at all. Dogs with severe stenosis may require medication and the prognosis is usually poor. Milder cases allow the dog to live a normal life.

These conditions can usually be prevented with proper breeding, a quality diet, and regular exercise. Other preventative measures include avoiding the use of Acepromazine, a common medication that can causes arrhythmia in Boxers.

Blood Coagulation Problems

Boxers may exhibit two forms of blood clotting conditions: Factor II deficiency causes the blood not to clot, and Factor IV deficiency is a lack of the production of the prothrombin, which coagulates the blood. Symptoms of this disease will cause frequent nosebleeds that are difficult to stop. Both conditions can be controlled with medication.

Digestive Diseases

Boxers are prone to digestive diseases such as colitis, pancreatitis, and pyloric stenosis (a genetic defect that causes the stomach opening to be too small, interfering with the normal digestion process).

Hip dysplasia

Like most purebreds, joint and bone issues can occur in Boxers. Hip dysplasia occurs when the hips develop abnormally and the head of the femur doesn't sit as it should in the pelvic socket. It is a debilitating disease that usually starts at a young age when they are still growing and the bones are being formed. This disease causes the right and left hind legs to become affected and it frequently happens because the muscles, ligaments, and other connective tissues supporting the hip joint become too relaxed.

The bones grow apart, instead of toward each other, as the ligament and capsule holding the bones together become strained and stretched. This misalignment of the hips puts pressure on the nerves, which causes the notable pain, symptoms, and signs associated with the disease.

Dogs suffering from hip dysplasia move more slowly and have difficulty moving their hips in any fashion. This includes simple tasks such as getting up or laying down, reluctance to play, walk, or use the stairs. Some personality changes may occur, as well as changes in appetite. Dogs may become depressed, because their quality of life has greatly diminished. You may notice limping and obvious stiffness while exercising or just getting up after sleeping.

Some dogs will never show signs of hip dysplasia, but early detection is very critical. A veterinarian will be able to examine your Boxer through observation or X-rays. There is no cure for hip dysplasia, but certain treatments can prevent or help with already diagnosed dysplasia. Some owners swear by joint supplements and/or only gentle exercise in those critical puppy stages where the bones are still developing.

The condition may remain steady, but many dogs will get worse as time goes on. The pain may be mild or severely crippling, and reputable breeders will have their dogs hip scored to check for signs of dysplasia. Since hip dysplasia is a such a common problem in dogs, wise and responsible breeders will not continue to carry on the bloodlines of those prone to problems.

Hypothyroidism

This condition is caused by the insufficient production of the thyroid hormone by the brain's hypothalamus or the pituitary gland. These hormones control the entire body, protein and fat metabolism, nerve and muscle activity, sexual health, and blood flow and the utilization of oxygen. Diagnosis may be difficult, since your dog could be exhibiting all the symptoms or only a few. However, the disease can be controlled by medication from your veterinarian.

Gastric torsion (bloat)

Medium or large, deep-chested breeds are most likely to fall to this ailment. When affected, the stomach twists trapping all contents and gases with rapid swelling of the abdomen. The pain will be substantial and immediate treatment is necessary. Gastric torsion can be fatal if not acted upon at once.

Cancer

According to a UK Kennel Club health survey, many types of cancer account for 38.5% of Boxer deaths. Boxers are most prone to mast cell cancers (benign tumors in the skin that become aggressive), lymphosarcoma (solid tumors of lymphoid cells), meningioma (tumors around the brain and spinal cord), lymphoma (malignant lymph tissue), and hemangiosarcoma (cancer of the blood).

Noticing symptoms as early as possible is key to preventing further severity. Symptoms may include weight loss, diarrhea, vomiting, issues with urinating, decreased appetite, lethargy, random bleeding or discharge, seizures, wounds on skin, swelling or lumps, and infections that do not seem to heal. Treatment is similar to human treatment, however dosage varies. Chemotherapy is commonly used.

Again, this does not mean your Boxer will have these ailments, there are steps that you can take with any dog and breed to help minimize the potential. Talk to your vet.

Recommended Diet

The diet of the Boxer varies. If you were to ask 10 different owners or experts on what to feed a Boxer, you may receive 10 different answers. The explanation for this is that there are so many different diets with great and bad results, and also Boxers can be finicky eaters. So you may have to do some research and experiment with different types of food to find out what works best for you and your dog.

One piece of advice commonly expressed by experts across the board is that you must let your Boxer grow at a slow pace. In those puppy years, where your dog is lanky and all bones, it is critical to feed at a steady and slow pace. Puppy food or growth formula foods with 26% or more protein should never be fed to Boxer puppies. Accelerated growth and too much weight on the bones will cause bone and joint problems. It is critical to never force growth in a Boxer by feeding them too much food or supplements to gain muscle. You greatly increase the risk of deformity and even death in doing so.

Finding a food that has a relatively low protein level of 23% or so, and a safe ratio of calcium and phosphorus is critical. In Boxer, excess protein can cause diarrhea and pack on more weight than their bones can handle. These dogs do really well on both commercial and holistic/natural foods, it's just necessary to look out for an acceptable ratio of minerals. Some experts may say to stay away from the commercial dog food brands, and instead go for the quality ingredients found in natural dog food brands. This much is obviously up to the owner and veterinarian, however it is unarguable that you should opt for quality foods for your Boxer.

Treats should be a part of your Boxer's diet, as well. Not only do they help with obedience training, but they are also a nice and safe change to their routine. Like kibble, dog biscuits should be free of wheat, corn, or soy in any form. These are just fillers and provide very little nutritional value for your dog. They are cheap and easy to make, but Boxers are prone to food allergies, and these ingredients are known to cause allergies is many humans and animals. Also avoid foods that contain by-products, and opt for foods that identify which specific animal they come from.

Interestingly, some known carcinogens are allowed to be used in dog foods. These ingredients include BHA and BHT, which are common preservatives, and ethoxyquin, a pesticide and preservative. Also avoid feeding your dog table scraps. Human food is usually high in calories without the nutritional value that dogs need in order to maintain good health. Skin allergies, obesity, diarrhea, diabetes, and other digestion problems may result from too many table scraps.

Boxers grow sporadically during puppyhood, so feeding schedules and amounts may change on a month-to-month basis. During the first 6 months of life, the puppy should be fed 3 times per day. At 2 months old, feed it 2-4 cups of food per day and increase this amount by 1 cup every month until the puppy is 9 months old. By 6 to 9 months of age, reduce the number of meals to two per day. Try to feed the last meal approximately two hours prior to bedtime. At 9 months until 1 year old, increase the puppy's food intake to 7-10 cups per day. According to the American Kennel Club, adult Boxers should be fed twice per day. Males may eat 8-14 cups of food per day, while females should get 6-9 cups of food per day. If your Boxer is highly energetic and receives a lot of exercise, increasing food is a possibility. For the size of the dog, this amount of food may seem too small, but they have a very slow metabolism.

Some common foods can be incredibly toxic and/or fatal to Boxers. These include chocolate, raisins, grapes, raw fish, and large amounts of raw eggs, garlic, onions, bread, pasta, corn, tomatoes, candy, and caffeine. Stainless steel bowls are recommended because they are unbreakable and do not harbor bacteria.

Highly digestible foods are a must and some experts may recommend a raw food diet, also known as BARF (Biologically Appropriate Raw Food). As with any raw food intake, there are potential dangers. It is critical and quite necessary to consult your veterinarian before partaking in this diet for your dog. It should also be known that raw food diets can be expensive and time-consuming. It is best to do your research and decide on which diet is suitable for you and your Boxer, with the guidance of a responsible veterinarian.

There are several foods that are harmful to any dogs, and these foods must be even more stringently avoided with small breeds, as they will have an even more toxic impact on them. Here are some foods to make sure that you avoid giving your pet.

Dangerous to Dogs!

- §Grapes and Raisins: These may impact your dog's kidneys and even lead to kidney failure.

- §Milk: Dogs have very little lactase to break down lactose in milk products. Ingesting these products can cause them digestion issues.
- §Onions, Garlic, and Chives: These can irritate the gastrointestinal system. Small amounts (which may be found in some dog foods) will not be harmful but it is best not to give large doses to your pets.
- §Avocado: This fruit contains Persin which may induce vomiting in your pet.
- §Chocolate and Caffeine: These may be a treat for you, but they are not for your pet. They can cause problems from vomiting to heartbeat irregularities to hyperactivity.
- §Macadamia Nuts: These may cause a strong reaction in your pet that includes, vomiting, tremors, and hypothermia.
- §Xylitol: This sweetener can be found in many foods, and is very dangerous for your dog. It can cause hypoglycemia as well as liver failure.
- §Alcohol and other Toxic Substances: Of course it goes without saying that alcohol, drugs, and other toxic substances should be kept away from your pup. Just like children, these dogs are curious and can get into anything, so make sure you puppy proof your house and are cautious about what you leave accessible to your puppy or dog.

It is always tempting to share a delicious morsel with your pup. For us, a splurge on a brownie means a risk of putting on a little weight, or throwing off our blood sugar, but to a dog it can be deadly. Always think before you share your food with your dog.

Even though we love our pets as members of our family they do have a different physical make-up and digestive system, and that is something that must always be considered. They do not need any additional food or treats to their regular diet. Also keep in mind that as short-statured dogs, putting on too much weight can be very risky.

Instead of sharing a it of your meal, take some extra time to play with your puppy, or offer something much sweeter than any treat, your affection.

Grooming

Boxers require very little grooming compared to most other dog breeds. They are easy going and easy to care for, and grooming is usually a fun activity for Boxers because all your attention is on them! You will be rewarded for the grooming with lots of love and devotion from your happy dog.

Boxers are a shorthaired breed with minimal shedding, however they do shed year round. Even in the winter months, it is beneficial to brush them daily or every few days, because any loose hair will just end up around the house. Maintaining their coat requires only simple brushing with a firm bristle or body brush. This will help loosen any dirt and hair, and it will help keep the coat smooth and shiny.

Bathing can be a difficult task for you and your adult Boxer. Larger Boxers may not fit very easily into a regularly sized bathtub. Fortunately, Boxers are not supposed to be bathed often as they can develop dry skin very easily. Too much washing of the fur causes stripping of the essential oils necessary for healthy hair and skin. When bathing is necessary, only use shampoo approved for dog use, as human shampoo will irritate their sensitive skin and make them itchy. It is also possible to use a dry shampoo, as it works very well for their skin, coat, and size. And it is also a lot easier for the owner.

To clean and take care of the teeth, you can get a special dog toothbrush and dog toothpaste and brush your dog's teeth. A simpler alternative is to give your Boxer a bone two or three times a week. Chewing and gnawing the bone will help remove the plaque and build up of tartar. If you prefer not to give your dog bones, brushing is essential to ensure good dental health and prevent tooth or gum disease.

Cleaning the ears should be a weekly grooming occurrence. Once a week, squirt an ear cleanser down into the ear canal and then gently massage the area just below the ears for a minute or so. As soon as you're done massaging, your dog may shake, so be prepared for a splash of cleanser to escape the ear. Then take a soft cloth and gently wipe the inside of the ear and down into the canal to remove dirt, debris, and any excess cleanser. Weekly cleanings will reduce the risk of ear infections, and you will be more likely to notice any changes in redness or irritation.

For many owners, nail trimming is the most difficult and anxiety-inducing part of grooming. If nails get too long, the dog will begin to walk on the back of their paws, which can cause an abnormal gait and lead to shoulder and hip problems. To clip your dog's nails, you will need a good set of clippers with sharpened blades or a rotary grinder to keep them short. To trim the nails, start by slowly taking a little off at a time. The nails should be short enough so that they do not click on the floor when they walk.

Having a bottle of styptic powder is also good to have at hand, as it will stop any bleeding that may occur from clipping into the quick. It is a clotting agent made of alum that works by contracting the blood vessels. If it is necessary to apply the styptic powder, simply apply a small amount with a cotton ball or cotton-tipped applicator. The bleeding should stop immediately. If this happens, your dog may be anxious about it happening again. If this is something you do not wish to deal with at all, many pet stores or pet supplier stores will trim for a small fee. Veterinarians will also charge a small fee for nail trimming.

Grooming your Boxer requires minimal effort compared to most other breeds, and the payout for having a happy, healthy dog is worth your time. The sooner you get your puppy accustomed to the grooming process, the easier it will be to groom him all through his life. The Boxer loves this personal attention and contact, so it is also beneficial bonding time.

Socialization

From 5 to 12 weeks of age, Boxer puppies will experience the stage where fear is imprinted. During this time, it is crucial to carefully and thoughtfully introduce the pup to a variety of stimuli every day, and to make sure that the experiences are positive. Instead of reacting with fear, you should encourage your pup to interact with new things, animals and people equally.

It is also important that you are able to control the new experience to a degree. Introducing and familiarizing your Boxer to new experiences will help your dog learn how to respond to and interact with these experiences appropriately and without fear.

The puppy mentality is most inclined to remember and accept new experiences between 4 and 12 weeks of age. Missing the window may socially handicap the pup, but the dog can still learn after unlearning. During this stage you should socialize your puppy, or dog, to people of all weights, heights, facial hair, people in hats, young children, other dogs and animals, and also odd items such as umbrellas, canes, wheelchairs, bikes, and laundry baskets. Watching and teaching your pup how to respond to passing traffic, odd and/or sudden noises are critical in managing his fear.

The dog brain is best described as a balance of dominance and submission. If not trained properly, your dog will try to dominate you, your family and other pets. To prevent this, you need to show your dog that you will protect him from situations that frighten him. It's important to make all social interactions positive experiences. Letting someone or something get too close too soon can cause a setback in proper socialization. Your dog may react by hiding behind you or aggressive growling. If this happens, correct the human, not the dog, showing your dog that you can "protect the pack" and that he does not have to.

Taking your pup on walks with a leash will offer opportunities for random socialization. Do not impose on other people though, and first ask for their help. Avoid dog parks during this phase, as it has a higher risk for disease and overwhelming aggression in other dogs. Start with small groups of people to ensure adequate socialization, and then move onto larger groups. Encourage good behavior with treats, praise, touch, and play to reinforce your dog's positive responses.

Reward the behaviors you want repeated and ignore or give a small signal to the behaviors you do not like. The signal could be "uh oh" or "too bad". If it does not seem to discourage the behavior, try a time out. Be aware of the signals you send to other people and animals. Make it obvious to your puppy that you enjoy encountering other people, animals, and things. Even puppies are aware of your actions and reaction, attention or lack thereof.

Understand when and why your dog shows fear, but do not reinforce this behavior. Cuddling, cooing, or coddling a pup or a dog when she is showing fear will not help the animal lose that fear. When your Boxer is able to see that you have control of the situation and that she does not have to be afraid, she will learn that you are the alpha and she will trust your actions and reactions. Teach not only your pup, but also the people in your home to never bother dogs when eating meals or treats, playing with a favorite toy, or resting. Bothering the dog during these times could make him feel threatened and/or prompted to bite.

You also need to explain that you are trying to socialize your pup to anyone who may help care for or anyone who is just around your dog. It is necessary for them to reinforce good behaviors in the same way you do in order for the pup to learn. If you are unsure an individual will abide by these rules, limit the contact between that person and your dog during the socialization and training stages. If left to interact with someone who doesn't follow your rules, your dog may stop listening to you and it could undo the progress you've made.

It is important to have your puppy socialize with other dogs. A good breeder will not allow adoption before 8 weeks of age to ensure they learn the core behaviors from mother dog and siblings. These include discipline, proper social play, and bite inhibition. Expose your puppy or new dog to other puppies and friendly adult dogs. Your puppy will be able to learn how to communicate appropriately with other dogs. If these interactions do not happen before they are 6 months old, they may become socially handicapped by sending inappropriate messages or failing to respond appropriately to another dog's message.

If one dog starts bullying another, you should intervene. A young, impressionable pup can develop defensive aggression if frightened by the dominant or intense nature of another pup or dog. With a calm firmness, interrupt undesired behavior the moment it occurs using brief time-outs. Do not use yelling and smacking, and do not punish the dog -- just a brief separation from the interaction is all that is needed. Good behavior and playing well with others should be encouraged with praise and small treats.

Taking a dog out in public to meet other people and dogs is an essential part of socialization. Unplanned meetings will show the dog how you calmly react to meeting a new person or dog. When dogs meet on-leash, keep the leash loose, as a tight restraint will encourage your dog to be tense, instead of relaxed.

If you encounter a dog off-lease, watch for body language. A wagging tail and relaxed posture are welcoming signs, compared to the worrisome signs of erect tails, raised hackles and staring. If you sense any tension, change your walking route right away or pick up your puppy and prevent any eye contact. Off-leash dogs are more likely to encounter danger and may also put someone in danger. Many dogs try to establish territory, so it is best to keep your dog leashed and/or stay away from unleashed dogs.

Instruct children to greet and pet the pup gently. Explain that puppies are not toys and they need to be treated with care and gentleness. Do not allow any rough handling, tail and ear pulling, poking, taunting, screaming, chasing that the dog obviously dislikes or any jerky movements that can seem threatening. Fortunately, Boxers are incredibly good with children; however, always supervise interactions between children and dogs of any age.

Training Your Boxer

It is essential for a dog of any size and breed to receive proper and humane training. This will benefit socialization skills, overall happiness, and your bond and relationship with your dog.

There are usually many options for puppy kindergarten and training classes in most cities. Not only will they learn many useful tricks, but it will also be a great opportunity to socialize with other dogs and people. Observe a class or two before signing up, and make sure to find a trainer that discourages bulling and dominance.

Obedience training helps puppies feel more comfortable in public with people and other animals. Learning new skills improves the dog's life, as well as self-confidence. Problems can result from energy and intelligence that is not being utilized to the fullest capacity.

Home training is also beneficial because there is usually less distraction. You must teach your dog his name, and to him that means, "look at me and pay attention". Using your dog's name in an angry tone may make him overtly fearful, and you need him to associate his name in a positive light. You should also teach your pup to come by calling him to you enthusiastically and rewarding the come with a loving stroke, a verbal "good dog", and/or a treat. Getting you puppy accustomed to a leash early on will help for future walks and social engagements. Use it every time you take him outside for potty breaks and walks.

Sometimes puppies will purposely or accidentally mouth or nip you, especially when they are playing. Let them know that it hurts and that they should not do that by making a "yip" sounds. Stop playtime when they bite, since play will reinforce the unwanted behavior. If they are not disciplined correctly, they are likely to continue this behavior. Playtime should include chew toys, in order to redirect his sharp teeth from your hands. Encourage gentle play, instead of play fighting, teasing, or roughhousing, because if they continue this behavior, they will one day be massive creatures that may be able to overpower you.

It is very important to proactively teach your dog not to protect his food and toys from you, any person, or animal. In order to do this, try removing his food dish at least once during each meal. Put an extra treat in the bowl before setting it back down to give the puppy a positive association with removing/touching his bowl. With toys, gently take the toy away and say, "drop it". Reward the pup for good behavior with a treat, and let him have his toy back.

Effective house training will require a little more time, as you should not leave your young pup alone for more than a couple of hours at a time. You need to be there when they go potty in an acceptable spot in order to avoid accidents, and so that you are there to praise him. If you choose to use a crate for your dog, never use the crate as a place of punishment. The crate should have only positive associations, which will make it easier to get your pup in the crate when needed.

Figure out ahead of time what rules you want to establish with your pet. Some questions you may ask yourself are, where will my pet sleep? What parts of the house are off limits? How do I want my dog to behave when company comes over? If you let your puppy sleep with you at night then you will have a constant bed companion. Your Yorkie may even whine and wait by your bed until you given in and head for the sack.

Remember anything you allow your puppy to do, your adult dog will also want to do in the future.

Pros and Cons of Breed

Boxers are famously known for their playful energy, however sometimes their energy is too much for some people. They need plenty of physical and mental exercise -- a minimum of two walks with training and/or games every day would benefit this breed best. An owner that likes hiking, walking, or jogging would be a great companion.

These dogs need ample interaction and socialization with humans. They do not like being left alone for large amounts of time, and do best with another dog. They need to feel like they are apart of the family, as they are very sensitive, emotional, and can be very protective. For the happiest Boxer, make them apart of your daily routine and treat them with love and care.

Boxers also produce a lot drool, slobber, and snot. You will often have these things on you and your all over your house. They have very thin coats, and do not tolerate extreme heat or cold very well. They are prone to skin allergies and genetic issues, unless bred well and fed a quality diet. Despite the amount of drool and dirt they accumulate, grooming is a relatively painless process. They are easy to take care of, however they require weekly ear, dental, and nail care.

Making sure you can afford adopting a Boxer is also important. Food, training, vet check ups, toys and other supplies will add up. An excitable Boxer could injure frail family members. The dogs themselves are also susceptible to a number of health problems, many which are debilitating and/or fatal. The usual life span of a Boxer is only 9 to 10 years, but with good breeding, healthy diet, and good medical care, some dogs can live longer.

If your Boxer develops a standoffish, skittish, or fearful personality, you could have an unpredictable dog in your hands. They can also experience separation anxiety when left alone too often, which can turn in severe destructiveness. When nervous, they can be aggressive towards humans and other animals. This may lead to potential legal problems. With adequate training, they are usually easy-going and mild-mannered.

Some experts could define boxers as hyperactive, however they are also lovable, friendly, and happy dogs. They are generally great with children and houseguests. They are known as "endless puppies" in that they are very goofy and will keep you laughing with their antics. Boxers as puppies, adults, and seniors all make very good companions.

Show Requirements

The ideal Boxer is a medium-sized dog, with a square-like appearance. He must have a short back, strong legs, and a tight-fitting coat. Muscles should be hard, smooth, and clean under taut skin. His gait and movements must look stride-free with energy and pride. The expression should be aware and his temperament dignified

When judging a Boxer, the first consideration is given to his general appearance and overall balance. Since the head and face is so distinct, special attention is also given there. Then he is judged for body components and gait.

Adult male Boxers should reach 23 to 25 inches, and females should be 21.5 to 23.5 inches at the withers. The males should also have larger bones than the females, both with a sturdy and muscular body. There is no size disqualification, so proper balance and quality of the character are of outmost importance.

The Boxer's body should be square in that a horizontal line from the front of the chest to the rear projection of the upper thigh should equal the length of a vertical line dropped from the top of the withers to the ground.

The Boxer's eyes must be a dark brown color of moderate size -- not too small, large, protruding or deep set --situated in the front. Expression should be intelligent and alert, with wrinkling in the forehead. The ears should be high and pointed, but cropped and uncropped ears are allowable. If uncropped they much be thin and moderately sized, laying close to the cheeks in repose. If alerted, they must fall forward with a definite crease.

The Boxer's skull should be slightly arched, without rounding or broadening. The forehead should have a slight indentation between the eyes and a distinct stop with the top line of the snout. His cheeks should be relatively flat without bulging, and they should taper into the muzzle with a slight, graceful curve. The length, width, and depth of the muzzle is influenced by the jawbones, placement of the teeth, and texture of the lips. The top of the muzzle should not be slanted downward, nor should it be concave, but the broad and black nose should lie slightly higher than the root of the muzzle.

The standard Boxer bite is undershot, with the lower jaw protruding beyond the upper jaw, with a curve that is slightly upward. The teeth and the tongue should never show when the mouth is closed. The upper lip is thick and padded, and the chin should be seen from the side as well as from the front. Any over lip obscuring the chin should be penalized.

The Boxer's neck should be muscular, round, and of ample length without an excess of hanging skin. There should be a distinct arch and a regal nape blending smoothly into the withers. The back is short, straight, firm, and smooth with the topline slightly sloped when the Boxer is at attention and leveling out when in motion.

The chest is fairly wide, with a well defined fore chest that is visible from the side. It should be deep, reaching down to the elbows with the ribs well arched, and extending far. His loins should be muscular and short with the lower stomach slightly tucked up, blending into a graceful curve to the rear. The pelvis is long, and especially broad in females. The tail is set high, docked, and carried upward. Undocked tails should be severely penalized.

The Boxer's forequarters are long, close lying, and not too muscular but firm. The dewclaws may be removed, and the feet should face forward with well-arched toes in a compact size. The hindquarters are strongly muscled with broad and curved thighs.

His coat should be shiny, short, smooth, and tight to the body. The only allowable colors are fawn and brindle. White markings are allowable, but must not be more than 1/3 of the entire coat, and should serve to only enhance the overall appearance. Boxers that are any color other than fawn or brindle, or dogs that are more than 1/3 white will be disqualified.

The Boxer should exhibit curiosity with a playful, yet patient personality. He must be alert, dignified, and self-confident. Any evidence of shyness, restlessness, or boredom should be severely penalized. The Boxer should walk with pride and a level back with a ground-covering stride. His gait should always appear smooth and powerful.